HAARA'G OPU

A Flower of the Heart

BENGIA ANTRA

Contents

PART II: OF THE EARTH

Acknowledgement

I would like to express my deepest gratitude to my family, especially my Aane, who always stood by my side and supported me to finish this poetry book.

Also, my sincere gratitude to Chow Piyaseng Manpoong Sir, for his unwavering support and guidance.

Thank you for always being there.

With heartfelt appreciation,

Bengia Antra

Preface

Poetry has always been my sanctuary- a place where emotions, memories and dreams intertwine. This collection, *Haara'g Opu (A Flower of the Heart)*, is a reflection of my deepest thoughts. Each poem is a fragment of my heart, capturing my relation with nature and the moments of love, longing, and resistance.

Every poem within these pages are not just words; they are pieces of my heart. And as you turn these pages, I hope you find solace, inspiration, a sense of connection in these poems while connecting yourself with the landscapes of emotion and imagination.

With gratitude

Bengia Antra

Earth

Whispers of Zephyr

She arrives by the winter's end
with soft curls of her,
her arms spread across the valley,
fluttering like wild butterflies in the sky.

The rhythmic dance of the falling leaves,
along the tender gust on the way
to the garden of dreams, where spring
awaits, with days of sweet melodies
and nature's gentle hum.

With the zephyr's magical whisper
heaven patters soft spring rain,
petals bloom in the drizzle of
zephyrous spring, gleaming with love
in the valley of dreams.

The Stories Never Heard

Flowing through the deep forests,
touching millions of lives at once,
quenching thirst on my path,
carrying the melodies of the winds.

I travel, crashing into mountains and
boulders, but never weary,
I travel on, until I meet my larger self,
realising the wholeness of eternity.

Through the paths, I travel,
I witness infinite stories, unheard-
of happiness, of adversity,
of excitement, of sorrow,
of dreams and the struggles, they sustain.

Along the way, I hear the sweetest melodies
of wings, flowers, leaves,
and the chasmic tunes of rain
make me dance to the rhythm.

Flowing through the mountains,

valleys and ancient woods,

I hear millions of stories unheard-

echoing through the ages of time,

to be heard and cherished.

The Fallen Sky

From afar, I saw the sky falling,
it was huge, rushing down upon the earth, sprawling,
with all its force, roaring through the air,
crushing all the lives in its path, laid bare.

The sky was wailing, unceasingly;
as a part of him was detached, grievously,
the force of drops drenched the soil
and the deluge came to despoil.

I couldn't rest anymore,
as the night had fallen, poor.
The thunders and the whispers the winds bore,
evoked a sense of restlessness, galore.

The stars were hidden behind the dark cloud,
the moon was lost to the night's loud,
and the night was darker than ever,
as if there were no tomorrow, forever.

In the dawn, I looked for the fallen sky,

with the first rays of sunlight, high

I calmed my breath, deep,

and looked for the dreams lost in a shadowed heap.

The Dying Tree

Through the window, I saw
a dying tree, once full of life,
striving to thrive a little more
with a little energy left within.

The baked leaves still sway
as they did before,
in the direction of the persuading wind,
until they fell to the ground, one by one.

The leaves ballet around
my windowpane like that
of a dancing girl enjoying
every bit of her favourite music.

I held some of them in my palm—
red, yellow, brown
and raised my sight to the drying branches
of a helpless and despairing figure.

It shed some more leaves,

as a sign of welcome,

to its guest for the last time,

before the departing wave: goodbye.

Dried and enfeebled limbs

still hold flamboyant birds,

just as the endless blue sky

holds the seven-coloured rainbow, fondly.

They sang the songs of birth, infancy, adolescence, youth,

the songs of lush green life, the misery,

and the songs of the final goodbye.

They sang the songs of racking departure,

and the melodies of blissful reunion,

until the only leaf detached and diminished,

promising to meet again in another life.

When it Rains

When it rains, I long for the past,
dancing guilelessly beneath the shower's cast,
among the innocent smiles in the valley,
that echo through the mountains, merrily.

When it rains, I drench myself
in the shower, to let my soul revive itself,
dancing tip-tap as it trains through the rooftop,
making my toes ballet over the top.

When it rains, the magical tones,
echo on the ground, the rhythmic notes
diffusing the fragrance of memories,
that hold the laughter of pristine infancies.

When it rains, it winds my soul with nature's spell,
making me sing along the drizzle so well,
beneath the endless symphony of raindrops,
my heart blooms as all worries quell.

Secret Melodies of Woods

In the woods near the waterfall
I saw a little flower, enthralled,
thriving in the shower, alone
under the canopy of nature's throne.

The pink petals smile,
embrace the gentle flow.
In solitude, they glow in balletic style,
dancing to the tunes of drizzle's gentle fizzle.

The green leaves whisper
the secret melodies of woods,
the symphonies of life in the meadows
that never sleep in the quiet shadows.

Nightfall in the East

In the east, I saw a lily,
swaying in the melody of the east wind,
under the reddish umbrella,
shining bright after the day's glow.

The shift of the shades in the welkin,
unveils the shades of the nightfall in the east;
harbouring the wings to rest,
yet the little lily was gliding and murmuring
in the colours of the evening.

The winds of the twilight flow,
gently tuning with the creeping dusk,
whispering the lullabies for the heads
waiting in the eastern garden to repose.

In the east, I saw a lily,
swaying in the melody of the east wind,
under the night sky full of life,
and tenacity to greet the rising sun's rays.

It's a New Morn

It's a new morn,
incredibly beautiful,
sunshine and morning melody adorn,
sweet chirps, delightful.

It's a new morn,
with a new story born,
day's beauty unfolds,
nature's embrace beholds.

It's a new morn,
radiates a positive smile,
with wings of joy, reborn,
God's gift, worthwhile.

Mynah

The sweet chirp meddles
my long-overdue sleep,
piercing the concrete barriers
of my undisturbed territory.

The starling's melody
flows continuously,
like an endless river full of life,
unfurling its magical water
wherever it flows, evenly.

The melodies of the Mynah
spread across my days-
dawn to dusk,
until it flies back to its nest.

The delightful, fun-loving bird
spread its wings to befriend me;
we touched our pinkie fingers,
signifying our promise of friendship forever.

Some days, I laugh my heart out
as it imitates me like a parrot,
and then it laughs my voice again,
eventually, laughing out together.

Can You take Me on a Flight?

Can you take me on a flight?
Through the winds, where whispers ignite,
beneath the canvas of this beautiful sky,
in the search of peace, where dreams softly lie.

Can you take me on a flight?
Between the clouds, listening to
the whistling breeze, flying high in
the sky to touch the heavenly colours of life.

Can you take me on a flight?
Between the high altitudes,
where mountains echo enchanting love songs,
and the untold tales of distant lands.

Can you take me on a flight?
Chasing the dreams of birds,
over the streams and waterfalls,
touching the colourful bow.

Can you take me on a flight?
Through the woods and rustling leaves,
between the poetic rhymes,
in the timeless phases of beauty.

Can you take me on a flight?
Wrapping my soul in your delicate and
soft feathers, where we'll soar
through the boundless sky together.

An Evening Melody

It sings me a song,
an evening melody;
of an ancient love and tragedy,
slowly and softly.

It chirps of the love song
when their eyes first met,
brimming with love,
unaware of the misery to unfold.

Love, sunshine, and
rainbows all along,
no time for sadness and
adversity, as love surrounds all.

The love melody turns into
a melody of melancholy,
and never-ending grief
when it saw its lady love
falling to the earth, lifeless.

It sings me a song,

of the uninvited guest

who shattered its life with his

inhuman and murderous bullets.

It sings me a song,

an evening melody;

of cruelty and beastly display

of blood and death.

It sings me a song,

reminding me of

how humankind is unkind

to them and destroys everything beautiful.

Moonlight Reverie

O, Moon, the timeless beauty!
Shining in the summer night,
shimmering with your silver light,
as bright as the gleam of a pearl
in the darkness of the deepest ocean.

O, Moon, luminous moon!
As your celestial light shines upon me,
I dream of wearing you as a crown
on my hollow dome, to conquer the universe.

O, Moon, mystic moon!
I wish to don shining pearls
on my forsaken neck in your absence,
reflecting your ethereal love.

O, Moon, the brightest in the sky!

The night is all alone without you,

so is my heart.

My eyes search for you in the dark,

longing for your magical shine

to fill the void left by your absence.

A Piece of Cloud

A piece of cloud high above my head,
floating alone among the clouds spread.
A little to the left, a little to the right
dancing along the winds in the height.

A piece of cloud high above in the sky,
traveling through the mountains like a spy,
a little to the down, a little to the up
smiling along the buttercups.

A piece of cloud just above the yellow flowers,
gazing at the golden garden for hours,
reciprocating the words of love,
promising to meet again like a beloved.

A piece of cloud high above in the sky,
showering the drops of love before the fly.
A little of sadness, a little of happiness,
dwelling in the life of wholeness.

A piece of cloud for me in the vastness

of the sky, touching souls as it sails high,

a little of love, a little of void,

painting hopes across the sky.

The Timeless Beauty

The beauty never seen before,
the elegance that never fades,
radiates through the ages,
whispers through the winds,
her gaze meeting with the heaven.

Like a mother, the green mountains
shields her lineage from harsh winds,
embracing them with love and care,
sheltering life within its bounds.

The land with dawnlit mountains,
a lap of hills cradling the first sunlight
of the country, dazzling and bathed
in the scenic beauty of greenery.

Sparkling like a diamond,
the snow-clad peaks stretch across
the majestic ranges of the Himalayas,
standing tall like a proud daughter.

The sleeping beauty,
Arunachal, my homeland,
my first love, where the sky kisses the earth,
and every sunrise brings a new beginning.

The rushing streams
wind through the mountains,
zigzagging, piercing the ancient walls
to meet the gigantic Brahmaputra.

Arunachal, where my roots belong,
deep in the heart of the earth,
revolving around the songs of the mountains
and rivers, whispering tales of ancient love,
echoing through the valleys and trees.

The Path I Walk Everyday

The path I walk every day,
for the past few years,
worn bare of grasses,
but of thousands of lives beneath.

The bared turf, the sole companion of mine,
walks beside me, regardless of the weather.
It doesn't change with season
like the people change their faces.

The familiar route,
a silent witness to the untold stories
spanning across infinite years.
And your secrets lie locked beneath the layers of dust,
lost in the world of unknown.

Like leaves fall onto the earth
finding their way home,
the barren turf guides me to my blanket,
with or without a human companion.

And on the day next,

it waits for me, ready to greet my steps,

as if it finds joy in guiding me towards

my destiny for the day, quietly.

Each day, the path beneath my feet

with countless steps of sorrow and joy,

bears witness to my emotions,

yet keeps my secrets in silence.

I Went Through the Forest

I went through the forest
as my mind ran hither and thither,
muddled around the confusing sphere
gravitating my thoughts to rest.

I went through the forest
looking for a butterfly on the way,
who bore wings of 7-colours
as I wanted to witness the best.

I went through the forest
listening to the tweets of birds
and whispers of the sanative winds
as I wanted to walk farthest.

I went through the forest
walking the tranquil paths
of peace seeking serendipity's embrace,
for I know beauty awaits my gaze.

A Walk to Remember

"Hoh Aan… dayato!!
(Grandma… wait!!)
Let me come with you,"
the old eyes saw me coming but
her small steps continued.

"No holo awden?"
(Where are you going?)
The wrinkled face smiled.
"I'm just having a walk,
come let's walk together," the dried lips muttered.

"Naam ngo awpub awyo bepan na…"
(I told you to not to go alone…)
The old eyes looked at me, smiling.
"I'm the queen here, nothing happens to me,
everyone knows me," she said.

"Mwlwnge?"
(Everyone?)
"Yes, everyone,
even these pebbles on the path
know me- the air,
the sky, the birds, everyone."

"Mwlwnge nage ajin ne?"
(Is everyone your friend?)
"Yes, they are my friends in solitude,
they know me better. I never had
any other friends like them."

"No bulam aagam goden?"
(Do you talk with them?)
"Yes, we talk sometimes,
we even share our secrets,
and they are good at keeping secrets."

"Halo no aab nyekam nan sanga ma den?"
(Then don't you miss grandpa?)
"I do sometimes, but you know,
life is to walk ahead, no matter
you walk with someone or alone."

"Hoge?"
(What?)
"You'll come to know when you grow old.
Keep moving, don't rest," she said.
Her steps continued along with her
best friend, the walking stick.

"There, that's the place
where we used to fetch water
before the pipeline was laid in our village,
we call it Kamcho," cracked lips smiled,
remembering the golden old days.

"And this is the place
where your grandpa used to sit and rest,
where the colours of the evening
pour their magical dust to relieve his tiredness.
Come, let's rest here for a moment."

"Donyi dulu namsi kaangamja"
(Sunset is beautiful.)
We exchanged our glances with smiles
on our age-gapped lips, deep breath, and
the magical whispers of the air.

"Come, let's go,

the chickens might be waiting for us,

it's time to keep them inside the coop.

They might be looking for us, common speed up...."

Songs of Fay

Just holding my breath deep,
pulling harder, to leap,
inch by inch, hour by hour,
each moment, I crave for the power;

The power to fly somewhere beautiful
where nature sings me melodies of serenity.
A place with no desire, only peace, bountiful,
where I can rest until infinity.

Sometimes, I just want to run away
up to the mountains forever to stay,
free of worries, hoping for a ray
to wake me up in the morning, with the songs of fay.

Up in the mountains,
within love's fountains,
where cats and dogs all around, cuddling,
speaking of love, we shine, twinkling.

The Frog and the Song

At the night's silence,
the frog jumped out of the pond,
croaking and cracking the bond
of the deepest slumber of the night.

I jumped out of my comfort
and asked the frog if he could end
the orchestra of disturbance, and
bring peace to the atmosphere.

The frog leaped from one place to another,
seeking no patience but
to sing his song of joy to me,
bound by impatience and a restless heart.

I shook my head in acceptance,
and he sang the song of joy,
song of happiness, of love, of friendship,
he sang and sang and sang through the night,
until his gaze met the first rays of the dawn.

The chaotic croaking of the frog

soon turned into a melody,

a melody never heard before.

I swiftly drifted away from conscious

to the unconscious world of melodies.

As the song soothed my drumhead,

I lost all the strength to resist.

As he sang more and more, and it worked

as a therapy healing my chaotic mind and heart.

Into the Eyes of an Owl

In the darkest night of the woods,
I stumbled upon an owl's wild hoot,
piercing through the wind,
wilder than the night's feral grin.

The arcane wind froze my senses,
spiraling through my nerves,
its grip tightening, ever stronger
as if it yearned to claim my life.

The mysterious owl spread its wings,
and perched beside me,
as if it wanted to speak to me
something unknown and otherworldly.

My gaze sank into the eyes of an owl,
I was pulled towards the swirling abyss,
inch by inch, restless and winded,
I was dragged deep into the unknown.

I woke up in the world upside down,

and found nowhere to go,

as everything swirled round and round,

and the hoots grew louder and louder.

I ran as fast as a flash

but ended up inside a room full of owls,

hooting and screeching, telling

stories I couldn't understand.

And it's been a while,

I couldn't sleep, as thousands

of owl stories drum in my head,

and still the hoots echo, relentless around me.

Of the Earth

I Lit a Candle

I lit a candle with crayons
in the dark night, hurting the peaceful
paper white with all my heart,
melded with the colourful wax pastel.

It burns vividly as I colour
red, orange, yellow, blue, and white,
beaming the dark room with
light and happiness.

It quivers as a man
in the middle of the storm,
as a sudden gust of wind flows,
striking my hair into the blazing wax.

The tall and watertight shape
bleeds watery as a child,
as the flame grows higher and higher.
And flattens as a solid, as if
given an ice cream in the summer.

I lit a candle with crayons

full of hopes stirred with

the motley colours of life in the dark night,

hurting the peaceful paper white.

Echoes of Home

Once again, I'm drawn back
to the old paths of my village,
to feel the magic once again,
to lighten my burdened soul.

The freshness in the air,
unfurls the love, ceaselessly.
The mountains and the rivers, all the same,
since I left them years ago.

Still the same smoky smell
emerging from the old wooden huts,
spreading through the path I tread,
and whispers the welcome songs in my ear, softly.

The aroma that tingles my nose,
still the same, the chickens and the bamboo
shoots, all mixed with wild herbs, the smoky scent of
the fire awakens my dormant taste.

The old wooden houses stand the same,
the bamboo walls adorned with decorative animal skulls,
whispering their untold tales in silence, while the hob
of dried meats remains unchanged.

The same aged-old culture,
the people, smiles, and gesture,
all are the same; what has changed is me,
a little drawn away by the external world.

Still the same mud-layered narrow paths,
but this time, I soak my feet in joy,
dancing to the rustling sounds
of fallen leaves on the sloughy ground.

Over time, city colours
overlay the image of my village,
yet the essence of my village remains unchanged,
rooted in memories of the past.

An Uneven Boxing Ring

A quivering sound of a woman
woke me up in the witching hour,
I dragged myself rubbing my drowsy
eyes towards the sound.

As I was approaching nearby,
the trembling voice
became more of wailing and crying,
begging for mercy in the name of *Love*.

And when I made to the spot,
I saw my father punching my mom
and she was only begging for mercy
inside the *Boxing Ring*.

Boxing Ring-
an uneven boxing ring
resulted out of their *failed marriage*
where superior showcased muscle power
upon a feeble body.

I was *Six*,
when I first witnessed
the uneven fight in the boxing ring,
and I'm *Sixteen now*, still witnessing
the fragile body getting wounded every night.

I, as a child struggled
between the life and the unending,
uneven matches in the *squared circle*.
Sometimes I wonder, if I will ever be able
to overcome this trauma in my life.

Oh! No...,
I cried, holding my mom,
I don't want to be in the *fighting cage*
beseeching and crying for mercy,
said my *fear of marriage*.

The bruises of *mayhem*
was still fresh on frail flesh of her
screeching her grief over the *dead love*
once bloomed under the bright sunshine.

Yet she *consoles* me,

with the never-ending

love stories

without the Boxing Ring.

Winds of Discord

Just another day, as usual,
winds of discord swirl as ritual,
finding solace in the lies they weave,
sowing sorrows in the heart that grieve.

Masked in different shades they hide,
finding joy in what they trade,
no mercy, no empathy,
the malice is the goal, no sympathy.

The fragrance of discord spreads so far,
piercing the hearts, leaving a scar,
wired in lies, they crave more lies,
they are the souls in disguise.

The tales of deceit, strong as a storm,
reaching your abode without alarm,
they take everything lovable,
do not even hesitate to be cruel.

Oh, human of the same kind,

what's the fun in being unkind?

Let's breathe together in peace,

I hope you keep the trash at cease.

Plethora of Whispers

The monsoon has come to an end,
and the August wind brings,
a plethora of whispers,
striking my soul harder.

It blew hot air balloons-
to shoot me down,
enjoying the paths
they have pursued.

I stood in silence,
and the heatwave blew,
frequently,
setting the whole forest on fire.

The scowls of the faces
lit brighter,
seeing the lives
burning in the deliberate fire.

I stood silent and calmer,

making my grip

stronger-

to the roots deep down my soul.

It took almost

my last breath,

suffocating my veins -

pale face and broken nerves.

I stood silent,

staring the whole forest burning

to ashes,

as I wept deep in my heart.

And as I wept,

the sky wept along with me,

moistening

the ash-burned earth.

And with the new dawn,

rays of hope grow

from the ashes

on the earth.

Pensive Me

Pensive me,
between the day's tumult,
I find myself adrift in thoughts.
Thoughts with no end and no beginning.

I find myself arduously wandering
across the rivers of abyss,
as every force pulls me deeper
into the gorge of deep hollowness.

I find people talking,
smiling and cheering each other up,
but I find no solace in the day
or in the nights, lately.

Pensive me,
just pensive me, drowned
in my own thoughts,
unable to voice my heartaches.

The Masked Call

Perhaps, it was you,
I couldn't recognise as the shadows
of the past were still visible in the darkness-
massive and overwhelming.

Perhaps, it was you,
standing behind me,
but I couldn't turn to you to say hello
as there were many masks around you.

Perhaps, it was you,
calling me to the paths, unknown,
pushing me to the edge, sharp as a blade-
hellfire, waiting to burn me down.

But it was me,
weeping in the shadow,
wailing on my own grave,
unaware of the life's reality.

Trauma

And when you think
it's all over,
the chaotic nights,
the tiring days,
and the colourless drops of emotions,

You fall onto the ground,
hurting your bared skin,
rivering out the claret
staining the gashed heart once again.

The search for peace,
in the middle of silent, lonely nights,
the brimming sights in the brightly shining days,
still drown you away.

Hello! It's Trauma at the door,
once again to doom you
to hell, with the chains of captivity,
and ceaseless affliction.

I am alluring as fine wine,

sedative as fine art,

engaging and absorbing,

all of you, slowly but surely.

Hello! It's Trauma at the door,

your friend in distress,

to take you to the dark,

silent, and chaotic world forever.

Hello! It's Trauma once more at your door.

It's Decemb'r

It's Decemb'r,
the month of stars,
of laughter, warmth and love.

It's Decemb'r,
the month of frost and fizz,
of chilling winds, all the
way from the Bay of Bengal.

It's Decemb'r,
the holy month,
full of prayers and blessings
for all in need.

Yet it carries,
the winds of Septemb'r,
bitter breezes that cut deep
into my skin, mercilessly,
to bleed every passing night.

Haara'g Opu

(A Flower of the heart)

A bloom in the heart's garden,
glimmering under dark shadows, hidden.
Timid and fragile like a foetus,
beneath the ribs, surrounded by the metus.

Thousands of dreams, bittersweet,
thriving little by little underneath,
through the wings of aspirations,
it glows like a child's smile, elations.

Budding desires, coy delight,
growing in the warmth of the moonlight.
Trembling in fear, its feet slide,
yet it dares to walk slowly with life's tide.

Bound to be a wish, merely,
it whispers through the window, dearly.
The dust of desire blends with the magical wind,
and kindles a light of hope in the dark, within.

Like the fire that flickers in the storm,
it stumbles against the people's norm.
Yet it crushes barriers behind,
taking the flight with its kind.

Beauty Innate

What could love ever do, if it isn't with you?
If it isn't with you, I shall perish beneath
the air that carries your essence,
dancing to the tunes of the love songs, you sing.

Like the soft warmth of morning sunlight
in the spring, spread across the meadows to
make wildflowers flourish, your love has
endowed me with boundless love and compassion.

If it isn't with you, I shall die
like a firefly ensnared inside the bottle of
hollowness, far from the darkness,
where loneliness and suffocation surround.

Like the colours of flowers bring
the vibrant shades merrily into the spring.
As such be thy love for me,
blossoming in the garden of my heart.

Shades of Grace

Colours,

as vivid as this world is,

yet it is incomplete

without the grace of *women*.

Every shade of life,

like colours on the canvas,

women paint our journey

with their vibrant shades of existence.

Colours and women,

like twin sisters,

bound together wherever they trek,

with no trace of recession.

Colours and women,

fragrance of love,

filled with devotion and

boundless compassion.

Colours and women,

though they may leave,

they leave behind vibrant memories

to cherish and embrace.

Last Pigeon

When there's no network,
no phone calls, and no signals,
still, I shall write to you thousands
of letters, without any sign of cessation.

I shall write to you every day,
to connect my soul with yours,
to feel the amalgamation of our love,
to conquer the world with boundless passion.

I shall write to you every day,
till the last pigeon flies in the sky
to the valley of love and beyond,
where our hearth and house awaits.

I shall write to you every day
until the last feather has flown its final flight,
until the last drop of blood dries,
etching its traces in the air that touches you.

Lost in Verse

Like the first rays of sunlight,

soft and warm,

like drizzle that drenches the earth,

like the first poem I read somewhere,

verses have that aura, elusive and profound.

Like a mother's embracing arms,

verses cradle my soul within,

gently lulling me into deep sleep,

guiding me through the paths of dreams.

Like a poem that heals the soul,

like a line that touches the heart,

I wish to be lost in that one verse,

or line that leads me to the land

of garlands of poetry.

A Word of Silence

A heart with thousands of words,
weighed down by unspoken emotions,
like a shadow that engulfs the bright
summer days, little by little like a creeping nightmare.

I yearn for a word of silence over speech,
as a sign of peace amidst chaos, yet
I stand alone, holding no solace in my grip,
and sob like a frightened child with deserted eyes.

Some days, I want to escape from this life,
through the mountains, rivers and valleys,
vanishing somewhere into the nowhere,
searching for the words that have never been spoken.

I chose a word of silence in the quiet night,
whispering to the shadows that swallowed my light.
They slip away like grains of sand through
my hollowed palms, swirling into the winds of lost words.

Magical Whispers

Through the night's window,

silence creeps in from the meadow,

she speak of no word,

but the songs of silent birds.

Draped in the wintry mist,

flowing mysteriously like a tempest,

she speak of no word,

but the magical whispers of verdes.

We breathed together in silence,

as our souls mend together in resonance.

We speak of no word,

as silence engrossed our bond, concurred.

Bundle of Joy

I found a bundle of joy,
when I saw a beautiful smile,
it radiated through the air, twinkling like
a star, casting warmth from afar.

An innocent smile that beholds
the beauty of grace and peace,
when one sees, they find heaven
in the tender smile of a happy soul.

The radiant smile of a child,
heals many broken souls, reigniting lost
hope as their hearts mend with laughter,
so sweet as a melody, filling heart with joy and light.

I found a bundle of joy,
in the smile of a child that beholds
the magic that lights up the skies,
where the fountain of happiness flows.

It takes me back to a time so pure,

when smiles resonated with happiness,

cradled in my mother's tender care,

unaware of the weight time carries.

Cradled in Dreams

Today, I just want to close my eyes and
fall asleep, as early as I can,
resting my soul and mind,
with heavy eyes, full of dreams.

Today, I just want to rest my head on
a soft and comfortable pillow of mine,
my friend forever,
and we'll fly high to a fairytale land.

Today, I just want to cradle myself in dreams,
taking refuge in a land of peace and comfort,
escaping the world
of dark and shadowy realms of life.

Today, I just want to close my eyes and
fall asleep, as early as I can,
so, I can wake up tomorrow as fresh as a daisy
and full of hopes like morning sunlight.

I May Say It's an Imagination

You say it's Orange,

I may say it's Red.

You say it's Blue,

I may say it's Green.

You say it's Tedious,

I may say it's Romantic.

You say it's Infatuation,

I may say it's Love.

You say it's an Illusion'

I may say it's an Imagination.

Imagination:

that bleeds enchanting love

and grace, making you

bleed more of love and admiration.

Reclaiming the Self

I shall not perish until I reach the shore,
until I gather all the shattered parts of me;
I shall not perish until I find myself,
amidst the chaotic storms of life.

I shall oar against the current,
to go forth and reach my destiny;
fighting the undercurrents and roaring waves,
just to push on a little longer in this saline life.

I shall not perish until I reclaim myself again,
until I surpass my distress and sufferings.
I shall not perish until I bloom like
a lily after the rain.

(Note** Kamcho- small traditional bamboo drip system in Nyishi)

(Note** An Uneven Boxing Ring- published in Arunachal Pradesh Literary Society (APLS) magazine in 2022